Praise for Chantel

"When I think of a positive role model, I think of Chantel Christie."

—LIL JJ, actor, *Just Jordan*

"Chantel is a great person, friend, and mentor."

—Tequan Richmond

In a World So Different

by Chantel Christie

In a world so different from any other
I hope to make some friends
In a world so different from any other
I hope to finally fit in
I hope that I will finally make it,
in this cold, cold world of hate
I hope to not be a misfit, I just hope to escalate.

This world can sometimes be a pain
Because of true meanness and hatred
Like teardrops falling down the drain,
Now I understand that I just can't take it.
In a world so different from any other,
I am truly determined to succeed
The feeling of hope is like a brother
and a new life I shall lead...

I Want to Live!

Chantel Christie

ILP
INFINITE L♥VE
publishing
REDMOND, WA

Published by Infinite Love Publishing
15127 N.E. 24th Street, #341
Redmond, Washington 98052
www.infinitelovepublishing.com | 888-733-7105

ISBN 978-0-9794827-3-1
Library of Congress Control Number: 2008934640

Printed in the United States of America
Book Design by Dotti Albertine | www.AlbertineBookDesign.com

Thank You!

*I would like to first thank God
who continues to bless me.
I would like to thank my family,
my publishing team, all my friends
and You, the reader.*

CONTENTS

Chapter 1

Exercise

IN OUR WORLD TODAY, youth are sitting in front of computer monitors and TV screens more and more, which adds up to hours of inactivity. Fast foods and snack foods are so much more abundant than when our parents were growing up. Food in grocery stores has a longer shelf life, which means the presence of lots of preservatives and sugars. All of this is causing an epidemic in overweight, out-of-shape youths. As young people, we are eating and snacking more than we are exercising. We're consuming more calories and getting less exercise, and thus an increase in weight problems—even obesity—among the youth. As we've seen on many TV shows, and unfortunately in real life, being overweight can spiral into other negative conditions, like low self-esteem, giving in to peer pressure, and many physical health issues.

So let's start exercising and moving now. The key is to not look at this as "Exercise." We need to find activities that are fun and that also take us outside into the fresh air. We can start with simple things like walking our dog or riding our bike; and, if we get involved with sports, we are going to get all the exercise we need.

The way I look at this, it's very simple. A lot of times, people who are overweight look upon losing weight and becoming fit as a "GREAT BIG UNDERTAKING." This doesn't have to be the case. Exercising, working out, getting active, moving physically are all ways to really help your body. It can be easy if you find something that is fun and that you enjoy doing, and I guarantee you won't look upon it as "Work." Obviously, if you put more calories in your body than you burn, you are going to gain weight.

So here's a list of physical activities that a person can enjoy. Pick one or more than one.

Get yourself an iPod. Put on your favorite music. And get started today!

Skateboarding

Skating

Walking

Running

Basketball

Baseball

Soccer

Gymnastics

Golf

Hula Hoop

Jump Rope

Skiing

Martial Arts

Playing with your brother or sister

Playing with your dog

Tennis

Volleyball

Dancing

Lifting Weights

Swimming

Hiking

Climbing

Chantel's TIPS

- HAVE FUN; don't look at physical activity as "Work."

- FIND SOMETHING THAT **YOU** LIKE: a sport or activity, or if there's a health club near you, join one!

- ALWAYS STRETCH! The more flexible you are, the more you'll feel like exercising.

- DO THE TEN-MINUTE WORK OUT PLAN: Pick five exercises and do them for two minutes each!

- DON'T PROCRASTINATE! Get started today!

And remember, this is just a short list. It's not every exercise that you can do. But it's a start.

I hope you guys will e-mail me and tell me about your progress!

info@chantelchristie.com

Chapter 2

Diet

WHEN I SAY DIET, I don't mean eating less. I'm speaking about nutrition: understanding the foods that we eat and what we put in our bodies. Your body is your temple, and you only get one in your lifetime, so make sure that you take care of it. We've all heard the phrase, "You are what you eat." For the most part, this is true. If we eat fresh fruits and vegetables, we will be healthier. If we eat a lot of greasy foods, better described as dead foods, they will catch up with us and we will become sluggish and, over time, our bodies will pay.

Here are some of my favorite foods: greens, macaroni and cheese, corn bread, fettuccine Alfredo and Caesar salad. As you can see, some of my favorites are greasy or fried, but in our home we don't overdo greasy foods. We try to have a good balance of fresh fruits, vegetables, and grains, but every now and then I still get my fried foods. I've learned a couple of tricks from my Dad about eating. One is to eat smaller meals more often which helps to take away the feeling of being hungry and then overeating. Secondly, instead of candy or an unhealthy

snack, he'll tell me to pick up a fruit, like an apple, orange, or banana. One of my new favorites is watermelon! And if you haven't tried it yet, wow! In small quantities, this is a sweet and tasty treat that contains a lot of water, which is good for you.

Now, for those of you who don't like eating vegetables, I've found a new delicious way to get the nutritional abundance that vegetables offer us: Juicing! My family began juicing a few years ago—vegetables and fruits both—and we've reaped great benefits in everything from weight management, to increased energy, and also healthy digestion. We juice carrots, apples, lettuce, watermelon, beets, celery, and the list goes on! Juicing is not only a substitute for eating vegetables, but it's also much quicker because all you have to do is drink. My family's favorite is a blend of carrot, apple, and lettuce. I hope you'll give juicing a try.

What about all the fruit juices and energy drinks that are out there? Look at the ingredients on the label and you'll notice that most are very high in sugar. Sugar is often listed as fructose or glucose. So, be on the lookout for these as well. Be a smart consumer.

The best way to hydrate your body is to drink good old-fashioned water. Your body will absorb it and love you for it. So will your skin, as water helps to hydrate the skin.

How much water should you drink everyday? Eight 8-ounce glasses is the most commonly cited daily recommendation. But this can vary from person to person. Nobody knows for sure and different experts have different views. Some say that you should drink at least eight glasses of water a day, preferably eight ounces or about .227 kilograms. But that estimate assumes a person weighing 150 pounds or about 68 kilograms, who exercises in some form for twenty minutes a day, and who lives in a generally cool environment. Not every individual meets those criteria. Not every person has the same water requirement. So it's difficult to apply a general rule. How much water you need depends on your physical weight, your level of physical activity in a day, and the environmental conditions. Often, it's a matter of common sense. On a hot day, when sweating profusely, we need to drink more water. Just remember that adequate hydration is a mandatory aspect of human life.

Here are some foods that are very tasty and healthy for you. From grains to vegetables, give yourself an opportunity to try them all.

Grains

Wheat Bread
Oatmeal
Granola
Nuts (Almonds, Peanuts, Walnuts,
        Sunflower seeds)

Meat

Beef
Veal
Duck
Chicken
Turkey

Seafood

Shrimp
Crab
Prawns
Oysters
Scallops
Lobster

Dairy

2% milk
Skim milk
Vitamin D milk
Soy milk

Goat's milk
Cheese
Eggs
Yogurt

Vegetables

Lettuce
Greens
Carrots
Celery
Beets
Cucumbers
Tomatoes
Potatoes
Onions

Fruits

Bananas
Oranges
Apples
Watermelon
Cantaloupe
Strawberries
Honey Dew
Pineapple
Mango
Papaya
Raspberries
Blueberries

Chantel's TIPS

- USE A SUBSTITUTE SWEETENER. Try honey instead of sugar.

- I like ice cream. But instead of ice cream, GIVE SORBET A TRY.

- TRY SMOOTHIES. Freeze fruit, put in a blender, add fresh organic fruit juice, and you could come up with a fantastic creation!

- FREEZE GRAPES and eat 'em like candy!!

- This is a SUPER SECRET TIP! Doesn't taste as good as apple juice, but it's good for you! BRAGG Apple Cider Vinegar. It not only helps you maintain your weight, but also helps you clean out your body. (I'll apologize now for the smell.)

Chapter 3

Education

THE DICTIONARY DEFINES EDUCATION as "the process of educating, learning, and knowledge." So in this chapter, I'm not just referring to education as schooling, I'm speaking about life lessons as well.

School will teach us most of the things we need to know in order to get a good job, have a career, and live a "successful life." For example, you need a high school diploma and a high enough score on the SAT/ACT entrance exams to get into a university, and at least a GED (general education diploma) to get into a community college. Almost any job that pays above minimum wage requires some type of post-high school education. I've looked at what it would mean to try to live on a minimum wage job and have decided, for myself, that I'm going to have to attend college. The minimum federal hourly wage today is $7.25. If you multiply that by eight hours a day

and then by five days a week, your gross weekly pay—before taxes—would be $290. Your gross monthly wage would be $1,257. Let's be conservative and say that my basic monthly expenses might be as follows: $600 rent, $300 transportation, and $200 food. (This doesn't include gas). After paying my basic expenses totaling $1,100—using *very* conservative numbers, remember—I would have $157 left over for everything else for the entire month: clothes, makeup, a coffee, ice cream, absolutely anything else. What if I wanna go to the movies? Or go out to eat? Or buy someone a present? What about getting a haircut? Or saving for the future?

When I look at numbers like these, choosing college is not a hard decision to make. And there are other numbers to look at as well. A college-educated person, on average, makes roughly double what a non-college educated person makes. I don't know about you, but I want the financial freedom that having a college degree can make possible.

COLLEGE VS. NO COLLEGE

Unemployment rate for
bachelor-degree graduates in 2001 .... 2.2%
Unemployment rate for
high-school graduates in 2001 .... 4.2%

Average income for full-time year-round
workers with high-school degree, 1997 to 1999 .... $30,400
Average income for full-time year-round
workers with a bachelor's degree, 1997 to 1999 ..... $52,200

Percentage of Forbes 500 members
without college degrees... 33%
Percentage of Forbes 500 members
with college degrees... 66%

When we talk about education, we should also talk about literacy. Literacy, as *Webster's Dictionary* defines it, is the ability to read and write.

I learned how to read at a young age through *Hooked on Phonics*. I found this a really fun way to learn. I believe anyone can learn to read. As I go through my teenage years, I see how very important reading is. I love being on the computer and I'm constantly reading text messages. One of my favorite things is reading books that take me to places I may never get to see—like Africa and China. I'm able to read about them in my own home, thousands of miles away. I can gain so much knowledge about other countries from just picking up a book and reading. Also, anything, and I mean ANYTHING, that you want to learn you can find in a book—from modeling, to creating video games, to learning how to play a musical instrument. It's all in a book. So I ask all of you to make reading a priority! Also, just a hint: if you start reading topics you truly enjoy, you'll have fun at the same time!

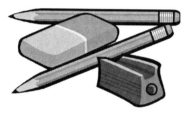

Writing represents the other half of literacy. This is something that I really enjoy doing. I keep a journal and write my thoughts and feelings down daily. Writing can teach you a lot about yourself. Sometimes I go back and read over my journal entries, to see some of my likes and dislikes, and also how I handled certain situations. Its fun, trust me! Because I'm a singer, I love another aspect of writing: learning how to write my own songs. To express myself, first on paper, then artistically through song, is truly gratifying.

Literacy—whether reading or writing—is something that we must take seriously.

Chantel's **TiPS**

- If you're having problems studying, try a tutor, or a learning center, like Sylvan or Kumon. I've experienced both and have found them extremely helpful.

- Try reading out loud, it can help with comprehension.

- "The dumbest question is the question never asked," my parents often tell me. So don't be afraid to ask your teachers questions when you don't know something.

Chapter 4

Sex & Pregnancy

S-E-X. SEX IS EVERYWHERE. It's in our face. Whether you see sex on TV, in the magazines, or on the internet, let's face it, society believes that sex sells. But, that doesn't mean that we have to sell ourselves at the same time. The internet has made it easy to have conversations with sexual predators, which is alarming and disturbing. We also have to be careful because when we engage in sexual activities, we also face the issue of sexually transmitted diseases (STDs), which we will get into in the next chapter.

When you choose to be sexually active, you may face many negative consequences. You put yourself at higher risk of physical harm and also abuse. Nowadays, a girl may be raped by her boyfriend. Being taken advantage of can happen when a girl chooses not to have sex. Sex is a very mature and intimate action. So when you put yourself in the vulnerable position of being alone with your date or boyfriend, you make yourself more vulnerable not only to rape, but also to peer pressure—doing more than you want to do. It is our responsibility as teenage youths to look at these issues before we decide to engage in sexual activities.

When you choose to have sex, it is a life-changing experience for a couple of reasons.

- **Mentally,** you've just passed the threshold of another first in your life. Now you will have to make decisions based on this newfound activity you have chosen to engage in.

- **Physically,** you're obviously not a virgin anymore. You are now at risk of contracting STDs—including HIV/AIDS—not to mention getting pregnant!

Sex is not something to be taken lightly. Some people can even become sexual addicts. Just like any type of addiction, sexual addiction is a habit that a person can find hard to break. And it can lead to other addictions, like drugs and alcohol, or even to prostitution. None of which are good, physically or mentally. Think about it. We make life-changing decisions everyday, which can change the direction of our lives forever. So when a decision about sexual activity comes up, we must make sure to thoroughly educate ourselves about this topic.

Obviously, abstinence is the best answer—not the only one, just the best. No one really knows when he or she is "ready." Educating yourself about sex is the only way to make a smart choice about whether or not to become sexually active.

Pregnancy and having a child, of course, isn't a bad thing in and of itself. But being unprepared can be. Earlier I mentioned mental health. Good mental health is a big part of a successful pregnancy and parenthood. I think people need to realize that having sex can also lead to having a child. Teenage pregnancy usually means having a child out of wedlock (not being married). This isn't necessarily a bad thing either. A lot of single mothers raise beautiful children. But it goes without saying that having both a mother and father offers a stronger foundation, as well as a broader perspective to the child.

I've talked about education, educating yourself about sex and pregnancy and also about the importance of a high school and college diploma. Once you have a child; it's not impossible, but it's much more difficult to complete your academic education—especially if you're a single mother. Who is going to baby-sit your child? Do you trust that person? Will the school allow you to bring your child? Will the baby be disruptive? "Distance education" on the internet might offer a solution to the teenage parent today; it can provide an education without having "to go" to school. You can get your education online, in practically any field you like.

Sex and pregnancy are experiences that at some point will touch almost all of our lives. Bringing another life into this world is not something to be taken lightly. There are many online outlets where you can talk or ask questions. Ultimately, though, please research and take sex and pregnancy seriously. See the Planned Parenthood link (www.plannedparenthood. com). They have a lot of information on both.

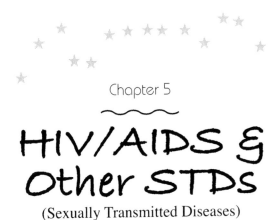

Chapter 5

HIV/AIDS & Other STDs
(Sexually Transmitted Diseases)

WITH THE WAY THAT HIV/AIDS is affecting our world, it has to be considered the most serious of all STDs. Being the United States Youth Ambassador on HIV/AIDS awareness is a position that I take very seriously. From the beginning I understood that I had to educate myself, and then try to help educate my peers. Even though I'm not infected with the HIV/AIDS disease, I still care deeply for those who have been infected or have caused someone else to be infected, and for the many people that will be infected in the future.

On the next page is a powerful poem I found while doing some reading on young people facing the reality of HIV/AIDS. It's titled *Friends* and is written in the voice of a young girl dealing with the difficulty of telling her peers that she has HIV/AIDS.

Friends

by Deanna

I want them
I need them
Everyone does
Without friends
The world would end
At least my life wouldn't feel
So empty and blue
Friendships help bring
Happiness, it's true
My life was a secret
From all who I knew
For 12 years I lied
To everyone I knew
Then one day I told
because I couldn't be me
I said I've got a disease
It's called HIV
No one believed me
At least that day
So I said it again
In a different way
Now the word was out
That this kid had AIDS
So many questions
So many afraid
Now they understand
That I am okay

And I have more friends
It's much better this way
When living a lie
It's hard to be
Myself or relaxed
In my friends company
Today I am happy
For what I have done
I told the truth
And now I can have fun
The kids in school
I can now see
They care for me
As a friend
With HIV.

HIV/AIDS has no gender or racial or economic lines. It is affecting our communities, our nation, and our world at an alarming rate! For example, it is estimated that 11.8 million young people, ages 15 to 24, are living with HIV/AIDS worldwide today. And, more disturbing, each day another 6,000 young people are added to these ranks, which translates to 250 new infections every hour.

American youth have not been spared. There are an estimated 40,000 new HIV infections every year with one-quarter of them occurring in youth under the age of 25.

For more information, I suggest the book *Teenagers, HIV and AIDS*. As I was doing my research, I found many books that will help inform you about this deadly disease. You can also go to the following websites: www.cdc.gov, **www.blackAIDS. org**, or **www.metroteenAIDS.org**, another organization I'm involved with based in Washington, D.C.

Of course, you can always go online to the search engine www. google.com and type in "HIV/AIDS information" in the Search field. I love watching all the music channels on TV that also present HIV/AIDS information. Check out MTV and VH1's websites: **www.mtv.com** and **www.vh1.com**. And go to www.bet.com to check out the "wrap it up" campaign. Get involved!

Global HIV/AIDS estimates, end of 2007

The latest statistics on the world epidemic of AIDS & HIV were published by UNAIDS/WHO in July 2008, and refer to the end of 2007.

ESTIMATE		RANGE
People living with HIV/AIDS in 2007	33.0 million	30.3-36.1 million
Adults living with HIV/AIDS in 2007	30.8 million	28.2-34.0 million
Women living with HIV/AIDS in 2007	15.5 million	14.2-16.9 million
Children living with HIV/AIDS in 2007	2.0 million	1.9-2.3 million
People newly infected with HIV in 2007	2.7 million	2.2-3.2 million
Children newly infected with HIV in 2007	0.37 million	0.33-0.41 million
AIDS deaths in 2007	2.0 million	1.8-2.3 million
Child AIDS deaths in 2007	0.27 million	0.25-0.29 million

More than 25 million people have died of AIDS since 1981.

Africa has 11.6 million AIDS orphans.

At the end of 2007, women accounted for 50% of all adults living with HIV worldwide, and for 59% in sub-Saharan Africa.

Young people (under 25 years old) account for half of all new HIV infections worldwide.

In developing and transitional countries, 9.7 million people are in immediate need of life-saving AIDS drugs; of these, only 2.99 million (31%) are receiving the drugs.

As staggering as these numbers are, they only represent HIV/ AIDS infections. We cannot forget about all of the other sexually transmitted diseases. One out of every four Americans between the ages of 15 and 55 catches one or more STD's.

STDS are transmitted through bodily fluids during sexual intercourse or oral sex if you don't correctly use a condom. STDS can also be contracted by contact with infected skin or mucous membranes, like sores in the mouth. Sharing needles or syringes during drug use, ear piercing, and tattooing can also expose you to infected fluids.

STDs are infections that people usually get by having sex with someone already infected. Most STDs can be treated and cured with antibiotic medicine. Some cannot be cured. But many of the incurable ones can be treated with medication to make them easier to live with.

It is very important to remember that most of the time you will never know if you are having sex with someone who has an STD. Anyone can get one. It has nothing to do with how "clean" someone is or how the person dresses and acts. Most people who get an STD, including HIV, are not aware that their sexual partner is carrying the disease.

So it goes without saying that you can look at a person who may appear "beautiful" on the outside, but who at the same time is infected with an STD. This proves the point that you definitely can't judge a book by its cover. So please be careful. And know that sexual abstinence is your best insurance policy for avoiding STD's.

Here are some of the more common STD's, along with a list of list of the curable and incurable STD conditions. Check out the sites at the end of this chapter for more information.

More Common STDs
- Gonorrhea
- Syphilis
- Chlamydia
- Herpes
- Genital Warts

STIS-sexually transmitted infections. There are over four million of them. A sexually transmitted disease is a sexually transmitted infection that has developed symptoms. The term sexually transmitted infection is used to reinforce the safer sex principle that you can't tell whether or not someone is infected just because they have no obvious symptoms. In fact, sexually transmitted infections are most commonly spread before symptoms—diseases—develop. For example, it takes an average of 10 years for HIV infections to develop symptoms and become the AIDS disease. The infection can be passed to hundreds of other people before anyone knows they've got it. There are more than 30 sexually transmitted infections, including, chlamydia, genital herpes, genital warts, gonorrhea, hepatitis, HIV,

HPV, syphilis, and trichomoniasis. Up to one out of every two people in the United States will contract a sexually transmitted infection during their lifetime.

Some Curable STDs	Some Non-Curable STDs
Chlamydia	Genital Herpes
Gonorrhea	Genital Warts
Syphilis	HPV (Human Papiloma Virus)
Trichomoniasis	Hepatitis B

CHLAMYDIA (kluh mid e uh)

Chlamydia is a common STD caused by the bacterium Chlamydia trachomatis. It is the most frequently reported bacterial STD in the United States. In 2006 over a million cases were reported to the CDC. Cases not reported are a big problem because many people are unaware that they are infected. Chlamydia can also be passed to a baby during childbirth. Chlamydia is known as a "silent" disease because about three-quarters of infected women and half of infected men have no symptoms. If symptoms do occur, they usually appear about one to three weeks after exposure. Chlamydia can be easily treated and cured with antibiotics. See below for symptoms.

Symptoms in Women:
- Abnormal vaginal discharge
- Burning sensation during urination
- Lower abdominal/ back pain
- Nausea/ Fever
- Bleeding between menstrual periods

Symptoms in Men:
- Discharge from penis
- Burning sensations during urination
- Burning and itching around opening of penis

GONORRHEA (gone or e uh)

Gonorrhea is a very common infectious disease. It is caused by Neisseia gonorrhea, a bacterium that can grow and multiply easily in warm moist areas like the mouth, throat, eyes, anus, and vagina.

The CDC estimates that more than 700,000 persons in the United States acquire new gonorrheal infections each year. In 2006 the rate of reported gonorrheal infections was 120.9 per 100,000 persons. Untreated gonorrhea can cause serious and permanent health problems in both men and women

In women gonorrhea is a common cause of pelvic inflammatory disease (PID). About one million women each year in America develop PID. The symptoms may be quite mild or may be very severe, including abdominal pain and fever. PID can lead to internal abscesses (puss-filled pockets that are hard to cure) and long lasting chronic pelvic pain. PID can damage a woman's fallopian tubes enough to cause infertility.

In men gonorrhea can cause epididymitis, a painful condition of the ducts attached to the testicles that may lead to infertility if left untreated.

Gonorrhea can spread to the blood or joints. This condition can be life-threatening. Also, people with gonorrhea can more easily contract HIV. HIV-infected people with gonorrhea can transmit HIV more easily than HIV-infected people without gonorrhea.

Several antibiotics can successfully cure gonorrhea in adolescents and adults. However drug-resistant strains in gonorrhea are increasing in many areas of the world including the United States. It is important to take all the medication subscribed to cure gonorrhea.

SYPHILIS (si fuh liss)

Syphilis is an STD caused by the bacterium Treponema palladium. It has often been called "the great imitator" because so many of its signs and symptoms are indistinguishable from those of other diseases. In the United States, officials reported over 36,000 cases of syphilis in 2006. Syphilis is passed from person to person through direct contact with a syphilis sore. Sores occur mainly on the external genitals: vagina, penis, or in the rectum. Sores can also occur on the lips and in the mouth. There are three stages of syphilis: Primary, Secondary, and Late/Latent Stages.

Primary stage: The primary stage can range from ten to ninety days with an average of twenty-one days. Usually you see a single sore (called a chancre), but multiple sores are also possible. These sores are usually firm, round, small, painless, and last three to six weeks. If adequate treatment is not administered, the infection will progress to the second stage.

Second stage: The second stage is most readily characterized by rashes, which may appear as rough, red or reddish brown spots on both the palms of the hands and the bottoms of the feet. However rashes with a different appearance may occur on other parts of the body, sometimes resembling rashes caused by other diseases. These rashes can be so faint they sometimes go unnoticed. Without treatment the infection will progress to the late and possibly latent stages of the disease.

Late and latent stages: The latent (hidden) stage of syphilis begins when primary and secondary symptoms disappear. This latent stage can last for years. In the late stage syphilis can subsequently damage the internal organs: the brain, nerves, eyes, heart, blood vessels, liver, bones, and joints. Signs and symptoms of the late stage of syphilis include difficulty coordinating muscle movements, paralysis, numbness, gradual blindness, and dementia.

Chapter 6

Thoughts Spawned

AFTER MEETING SOME WONDERFUL and inspiring people at Metro Teen AIDS in Washington D.C., through my HIV/AIDS ambassadorship, many thoughts began to come into my mind. I found myself researching this topic and some of my thoughts turned into poems and spoken word. I was also able to read the beautiful words of others in the face of such adversity. It truly opened my eyes.

On the following page is one of my poems.

Nothing to Lose
by Chantel Christie

I want him, but he wants her.
I see them together and, man, does it hurt.
When we broke up, he said, "We'll always be friends."
"'Of course," I agreed. "Best Friends till the End."
They had their one-year anniversary that day.
And somehow I managed to say,
"I'm happy for you both. You are a beautiful pair."
I said, "Sorry, But I have to go."
I needed some air.
Tears started to flow, mascara began to run.
The clouds came out and covered the sun.
Thinking why can't I have my prince in shining armor?
But what doesn't kill me will only make me stronger.
Out he came; to see what was wrong.
I said, "Nothing at all, tonight I'll call you on the phone."
He replied, "No, I've known you for years.
And if nothing's wrong
Then why all the tears?'
I told him that ending our relationship was a mistake.
I didn't want it to happen.
And it was causing me pain that I couldn't take.
Then he told me the real reason he had to let me go.
He thought that it was time that he let me know
At first he couldn't say it
Because even he was scared.
He didn't wanna tell me;

Cause it was something he feared.
He reached in his coat pocket;
Came out with a piece of paper.
He said, "Before you open it,
I just wanna thank you.
You were always there when I needed someone
And regardless of anything, you'll always be my perfect one."
Another tear fell as I unfolded the paper.
I couldn't understand what all the words meant.
Until I saw that word and had a silent fit.
I asked who wrote this?!
And what did it mean?
He said, "It's mine, I'm just a statistic teen."
I said, "So, what your telling me is that you have this?!"
Wait, Wait, Wait. I can't grasp this!
He said, "I love you and want you,
but there's nothing I can do.
As you can see I'm positive
And I don't wanna give it to you."
HIV was the word inked on paper.
He said, "'If you had it, you'd understand;
there's no way they can save you."
I didn't understand.
It's just over like this?!
He put his hand to his mouth and blew me a kiss.
He said, "I cared about you too much
to live silently with this disease.
I know you won't get over it easily, but please,
Once you move on, please have SAFE sex.

Because the day I was diagnosed,
Is a day I will never forget."
He left me standing there
with thoughts rushing through my mind.
One of them was, "Man, he's one of a kind."
To love me enough to leave me, even though it hurts.
He did it to protect me.
And yes, it worked.
I never figured out why he picked her
if he was HIV positive.
But I guessed it was because she was too.
And neither had anything to lose.

Chapter 7

Teenage Suicide

TEENAGE SUICIDE IS SOMETHING that is very alarming and the numbers are on the rise. It seems as though many youth feel they have no way out, so they decide to end their lives—an unfortunate trend we are seeing in our world today. Teenage suicide has also now become more of a public display of violence. In high schools, middle schools, and even in some grade schools, students have been found carrying weapons to school. One of the biggest and most documented cases is the Columbine High School shooting.

On Tuesday, April 20, 1999, at Columbine High School in Columbine, an unincorporated town in Jefferson County, Colorado, near Denver, two teenage boys embarked on a shooting rampage, killing twelve students and a teacher, as well as wounding twenty-three others, before committing suicide. It was the fourth-deadliest school killing in United States history, after

the 1927 Bath School disaster, the 2007 Virginia Tech massacre, and the 1966 University of Texas massacre. Columbine has been the deadliest high school shooting to date.

With new gun laws being more lenient, the ability to gain access to a firearm in the home is something that is very scary. A lot of times guns in the home are not properly stored by the parent or adult. Legally, guns are supposed to be locked away, out of the reach of minors. When they are not, as we've seen, the outcome can be catastrophic.

Teen suicide statistics draw a correlation between gender and suicide. It is interesting to note that there are some very clear indications that suicide is different for males and females, attempted and completed suicides alike. For example, males are four times more likely to die from suicide than females. However, teen girls are more likely than teen boys to attempt suicide. So, even though teenage girls make more attempts on their own lives than teenage boys, the boys are more likely to actually complete a suicide attempt. Because the suicide completion rate is higher in boys, because their attempts are less likely to be a "call for help," there is often little opportunity for intervention, or to get males into treatment.

Risk factors for teenage suicide:
Teen suicide statistics offer a look at the most likely causes of teen suicide. Some of the strongest teenage suicide risk factors include the following:

1. Aggressive behavior
2. Disruptive behavior
3. Substance abuse
4. Depression

These risk factors play on the often tumultuous feelings experienced by teenagers. Intense emotions can contribute to a teen's sense of helplessness and to a general feeling that life is not worth living. Adults taking these feelings seriously is an important part of preventing teen suicide.

Another risk factor to consider is the presence of firearms. Because firearms are used in more than half of teen suicides, it is important to realize that easy access to a firearm and ammunition can contribute to a teenage death by suicide. Teenagers who express suicidal thoughts and feelings should not have ready access to firearms.[9]

Suicide can be caused by depression amongst other things. Not to mention, with our world moving so fast, no one is taking the time to truly listen and get to know each other. A lot of the time, youth are crying out for help. But the cries go unheard, the signs unaddressed or unnoticed by peers, teachers, and even parents.

There are so many things to live for. The air we breathe, the trees, the sun, our families, the beauty of Mother Nature—and besides, life is as fun as you make it. I truly hope and pray that any teen out there reading this book and who may be having suicidal urges or thoughts reaches out for help. As a teen myself, I've already witnessed suicide, up close and personal. Although a traumatic experience, losing someone I loved so much, the situation helped me grasp an alarming epidemic that confronts all of us. My life was touched in a way that I find hard to put into words. You wish you could have talked to the person. You wish you could have helped the person in some way. But since it was not to be, we try to move on. We come together as a family to help each other through the hard times. So many lives are affected by a suicidal act. With so much for all of us to live for, my dream is that, as a society, we try to help at-risk teens.

Teen Suicide Prevention Hotline
http://www.suicide.org/teen-suicide-and-youth-suicide.html
http://www.jaredstory.com/suicide.html
http://www.teachhotline.org/

Chapter 8

Living Your Dreams

EVERY DREAM IS ATTAINED by following goals you set for yourself. This chapter may well be my favorite, as I live out my dreams on a daily basis, from writing this book to finishing my album titled "My Dream". You can find the album on my website: www.chantelchristie.com.

Through a process I call "Chani's Dream Plan," I've watched my dreams come to life, which tells me that anything is possible! When you look at your dream to do something, it can seem overwhelming. My mother has always taught me to make lists and to complete them. This is one of the best ways I've learned to achieve my goals, thus my dreams.

A person's dreams don't have to be becoming an author, a singer, or a superstar athlete. A person can dream of being a gardener, architect, or maybe of obtaining a college degree. The best thing about any dream you have is that most are attainable and they are all yours!

For instance, Oprah Winfrey's dream led her to become the first African-American woman to own her own television network. Bill Gates dropped out of college to follow his dream, which led him to become the founder of Microsoft and the richest man in the world. These are people who had a dream, saw their opportunity, and seized the moment to make their dreams a reality. Stories like theirs inspire us all. Not to mention the story of Barack Obama, who may become the first African-American president in history—a dream so lofty as to be thought unattainable until now.

Following and living your dreams is what life is all about. It gives you something to strive for. Setting goals and attaining them step by step, will give you a sense of accomplishment. You owe it to yourself to dream big. You can truly do anything in life that you choose if you are determined and willing to sacrifice the time necessary to accomplish your goals. So good luck, my friends, in trying to make all of your dreams come true.

Dreamin'

by Chantel Christie

Dreamin' of the day I'll hit the stage
Fans yelling! screaming my name
Applause erupts, a smile upon my face
Adrenaline pumping!!! My mind in a haze
I've waited for this day for fifteen years!
Put in hard work, blood, sweat and tears
No one can stop me
I'm making the impossible, possible
No one can stop me
I'm literally unstoppable
I've given up so much
Because I was determined to make this dream come true.
Family and friends believing in me, they all came through.
I look into the crowd, there goes Angelique
I look next to Skye, and there's Gigi!
Little Dougie posted in a front row seat
I finish my set, everyone jumps to their feet
Cheering and clapping
All for me
Then all of a sudden
Everything vanishes
I'm back to reality
In the studio working on a song called "Who is she"
I guess I was just dreamin', to put it simply...

Chantel's DREAM PLAN

- GOALS: Setting specific, attainable targets that will help make your dream a reality

- FOCUS: Mental concentration on your goal

- DRIVE: The yearning inside to accomplish your goal

- DETERMINATION: The willingness to see your goal achieved

- HARD WORK: The work necessary to attain your goals.

Chapter 9

Self-Love

TO ME, SELF-LOVE SPEAKS about self-esteem and self-respect. It's not about being self centered but, rather, loving yourself and trying to do the best that you can without tearing yourself down, or trying to live up to someone else's idea of what you should be, what you should look like, how you should dress, or how you should talk. We are all different but, ultimately, self-love is what makes us all special and beautiful in our own right.

Finding self-love is about being happy with you. Not letting your peers, or what you read in magazines, or see on television make you believe that you have to be something or someone that you're not. When you look in the mirror, being happy with yourself is all that matters. The reflection that you see is just an outward appearance. The beautiful person inside is the person you have to find through self-love. Once you find self-love, everything else will fall right into place. It's just like in business, "If you believe in your product, eventually so will the consumer." On the other hand, if you say to yourself "I'm ugly" or "There's just something wrong with me," sooner or later you are going to begin to believe it, and so will others.

On a daily basis, as we watch television, read fashion magazines or look on the internet. We don't see images that reflect ourselves. What we see is society's idea of what's beautiful or what happens to be the latest in-thing: people with perfect skin, people in perfect shape, people who live perfect lives, or who seem to live better lives than ours. If we're not careful, all of these images can lead to negative thoughts and cruel self-talk. Self-love can help us out with the constant bombardment of unrealistic images. Self-love can protect us and let us know that they are just that—manufactured images—and no more. We need to love ourselves enough to know that we are special and beautiful in our own right. I love watching TV and surfing the net, but I also love myself enough to know that this is just entertainment. I will not compare myself to the people on the screen to the point that I begin to hurt myself.

Self-love is inner happiness—in other words, being content and happy with the person that you are becoming day-to-day. It's a beautiful thing to love yourself. And to all my friends out there, I truly hope that you do love yourself, because that will allow you to love others. I'M SENDING MY LOVE TO YOU ALL!

Chantel's TIPS To Finding Self-Love

- DON'T COMPARE yourself to others.

- Remember YOUR BODY IS YOUR TEMPLE. So treat it the best that you can with healthful food and exercise.

- GIVE YOURSELF 15 MINUTES A DAY FOR YOURSELF. Sit down and meditate or just enjoy nature, take a walk or sit under a tree.

- WATCH WHAT YOU SAY TO YOURSELF. Try to only give yourself positive reinforcements, like "I love myself", "I am good enough," "I'm not fat," "I'm not too skinny," "God made me perfect."

- YOUR OUTWARD APPEARANCE DOESN'T DEFINE YOU, not your hair, your weight, or your clothes.

REMEMBER WE ARE ALL BEAUTIFUL PEOPLE!

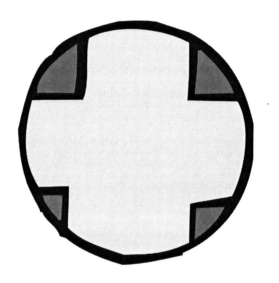

Chapter 10

Top 5s

TOP 5'S ARE MEANT TO BE FUN. So I decided to let you all in on some of my PFT's (personal favorite things). I couldn't pick more than five, or else this chapter would've gone on forever! Maybe we share some of the same interests, so don't be afraid to e-mail me at **info@chantelchristie.com** with YOUR top 5s!! I'd love to hear from you.

Causes & Organizations
1. HIV/AIDS Awareness
2. YMCA Youth Programs
3. Literacy Programs
4. Leukemia Society
5. American Red Cross

Male Musicians

1. Chris Brown
2. Justin Timberlake
3. Kanye West
4. Lil Wayne
5. Andre 3000

Female Musicians

1. Alicia Keys
2. Tynisha Keli
3. Beyonce
4. Selina Gomez
5. Karina Pasian

Male Hip Hop

1. Andre 3000
2. Kanye West
3. Lil Wayne
4. P. Diddy
5. Jay Z

Female Hip Hop

1. Lil Mama
2. Chani
3. Lady Sovereign
4. Aaliyah
5. Ciara

Male Pop

1. Michael Jackson
2. Prince
3. Justin Timberlake
4. Maroon 5
5. Jesse McCartney

Female Pop

1. Rihanna
2. Fergie
3. Jordin Sparks
4. Madonna
5. Natasha Bedingfield

R&B

1. India Arie
2. Alicia Keys
3. Monica
4. Brandy
5. Chani

Blues

1. Ray Charles
2. B.B King
3. Eric Clapton
4. Jimi Hendrix
5. Stevie Ray Vaughn

Rock

1. Avril Lavigne
2. Linkin Park
3. Blink 182
4. OneRepublic
5. Maroon 5

Gospel

1. Mary Mary
2. Kirk Franklin
3. Marvin Sapp
4. Natalie Grant
5. Switchfoot

Food
Specifics
1. Chicken tacos
2. Collard greens
3. Macaroni and cheese
4. Corn Bread
5. Fettuccine Alfredo with chicken

Type
1. Italian
2. Soul food
3. Chinese
4. Jamaican
5. Mexican

Desserts
1. Banana Pudding
2. Peach Cobbler
3. Apple Crumb Pie
4. Tiramisu
5. Sweet Potato Pie

Ice Cream/ Sorbets
1. Chocolate Chip Cookie Dough
2. Neapolitan
3. Jamoca
4. Raspberry Sorbet
5. Mango Sorbet

Herbal teas
1. Green
2. Chamomile
3. Throat Coat
4. Ginger
5. Raspberry

Tennis Shoes
1. Vlado
2. Adidas
3. Converse
4. Air Jordans
5. Nike

Heels
1. Manolo Blahnik
2. Jimmy Choo
3. Marciano
4. Prada
5. BeBe

Stores
1. Forever 21
2. H&M
3. Urban Outfitters
4. Ed Hardy
5. Target

Travel
1. Mexico
2. Italy
3. Paris
4. Africa
5. Japan

Pets
1. Dogs
2. Cats
3. Fish
4. Hamster
5. Rabbit

Dogs
1. Tea Cup Poodle
2. Golden Retriever
3. Yorkshire Terrier
4. Pit bull
5. Pugs

Favorite colors
1. Pink
2. Red
3. Blue
4. Lime green
5. Black

Places to go on the Net
1. Myspace.com
2. Youtube.com
3. iTunes
4. LimeWire
5. Myspace.com/mychani

Movies
1. Enough
2. Life
3. Crash
4. Love and Basketball
5. Juno

Videos
1. Like You'll Never See Me Again - Alicia Keys
2. Homecoming - Kanye West
3. No Matter What - T.I.
4. Heaven Sent - Keyshia Cole
5. With You - Chris Brown

TV shows
1. Tyra (all)
2. Oprah
3. First 48
4. Baldwin Hills
5. CNN

Cartoons

1. Gullah Gullah Island
2. Tom & Jerry
3. Jimmy Neutron
4. Flintstones
5. As Told by Ginger

Sitcoms

1. Fresh Prince of Bel Air
2. Family Matters
3. The Cosby Show
4. Boy Meets World
5. Three's Company

Cars

1. Hybrids
2. Range Rover
3. Mercedes Benz
4. 66' Mustang Convertible
5. Hummer

Books

1. *The A-List*
2. *Harry Potter*
3. *I Want to Live: A Teenager's Guide to Finding Self-Love*
4. *Letters to A Young Brother*
5. *Malcolm X: Autobiography*

Birthday themes

1. Midnight in Paris
2. Paris Tokyo
3. Hollywood
4. Hawaiian Luau
5. Summer Beach Party

Makeup Suppliers

1. MAC
2. Sephora
3. N.Y.C.
4. K.L.S.
5. Neutrogena

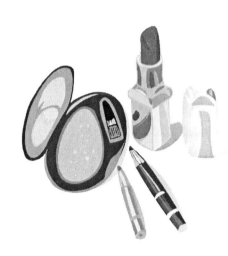

Nail Polish

1. Nicole
2. Sinful Colors
3. OPI
4. Maybelline
5. MAC

Exercises

1. Dancing
2. Cardio
3. Pushups
4. Crunches
5. Meditating

Designers
1. Marciano
2. Juicy Couture
3. Chanel
4. Heatherette
5. Lauren Conrad

Quotes

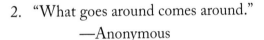

1. "Everything happens for a reason."
   —Anonymous

2. "What goes around comes around."
   —Anonymous

3. "I hear and I forget. I see and I remember. I do and I understand."
   —Confucius

4. "One good thing about music, when it hits, you feel no pain."
   —Bob Marley

5. "If you do what you've always done, you'll get what you always got."
   —Anonymous

Chapter 11

I Want to Live

I want to live
by Chantel Christie

Get on this highway
It has speed bumps
Road Blocks
And construction work ahead
Take from it what you may
But as I set out on this journey,
I'm gonna take you through this town called life

It's sad to see
But it's a reality
I take a left at the light
Head down two blocks
I see a teen on the corner

She has a baby on her hip
And one in her stomach
Got knocked up with no father in sight

Sad to see,
But it's a reality
I go two more miles
And I see an old man with back pains
Should've changed his life way back in the day

Sad to see
But it's a reality
Sign said DETOUR AHEAD
I pass Planned Parenthood
A young man stands outside
Looking as if he's seen a ghost
HIV positive;
He was just diagnosed

Sad to see
But it's a reality
A woman walked by looking sickly
She said, "Join the crowd.
"Look what one night of silly partying did to me."
She had Syphilis
And all she could ask herself was,
"How did I get tricked into this?"
But it was all too late
She had made her mistake

Sad to see
But it's a reality
I accelerate my speed and keep rolling down the block
I see a squad car and two police officers
Right across the street are young men selling drugs

Sad to see
But it's a reality
As I pause before getting on the highway
I look to my right and see a woman
She's strung out on drugs
Shaking my head; I think What a crazy situation
If only she hadn't ignored the signs
With such a brilliant mind
She could've been a part of a huge company
Or even owned a hair salon
That was her dream
But now her dream is gone
Formula, Diapers, Daycare
Feed them, Bathe them, and Find them something to wear
It is her daily ritual, No way to step outside the box

Sad to see
But it's a reality
I think about my childhood best friend
Look out the window
And speak of the devil
There he went
He had a sharp object in his hand

With tears streaming down his face
Radio reports say a young man
committed suicide later on that day
Thoughts flooded my mind,
what if I would've stopped to help?
Been a real friend?
Maybe he wouldn't be lying in the morgue
He felt as though he had no one
And was full of mind boggling emotions
He left a note, it said, "I'm sorry"
It was typical of him,
Always to apologize for something
He didn't owe an apology
If only someone had been there for him
But I guess when it's your time to go;
You're gone. No second thoughts. No second chance
Your family has to let go; No second glance

It's sad to see
But it's a reality
As I pull into my driveway
I see my neighbor
She has a teen daughter
With low self-esteem
She was a little overweight
And they didn't want her on the cheerleading team
So she came home from school, tears in her eyes
Ran up the stairs,
without giving her mom a chance to say goodbye

I think we all know what happened in the bathroom that day
She committed suicide; She saw no other way
She was unhappy and left her family in pain
But she felt if she went to heaven, Peace, she would gain

Sad to see
But it's a reality
I go into my home
And recount all the horrifying things I saw today

Sad to see, Yes
But it's a reality
We walk around blind to the problems
and epidemics that face us
We walk past and ignore situations
that will forever change us
Everyone has a dream and Everyone has aspirations
Even if you're not in the best situation
Let go and let god
Be focused and determined
And Give it all you've got
You don't have to be a statistic
And neither do I
Lets all ban together
With only tears of joy in our eyes
Life is to Live
And Living is Life
But at the gates of heaven
At least you'll know you tried

You need to learn
From the mistakes of others
You won't live long enough to make them all yourself
Don't do drugs or get an addiction,
to where you're in need of help
Be independent stand on your own two feet
And smile every night before you go to sleep
Look in the mirror every morning and say
"Yes I'm beautiful
God made me what I am,
At the end of the day he loves me for me."

So stand strong,
and make the right choices
I don't know about you but,
I WANT TO LIVE!

References

http://www.csgnetwork.com/humanh2owater.html

http://www.forbes.com/2003/07/28/cx_dd_0728mondaymatch.html

http://www.BlackAIDS.org

http://www.CDC.gov

http://www.youngwomenshealth.org/std-general.html

http://www.teensuicide.us/articles1.html

http://www.thehelpline.org

http://www.MetroTeenAids.gov

http://www.plannedparenthood.com

PHOTO CREDITS

john&joseph photography | www.jkhptoto.com

derek blanks | www.dblanks.com

Chani is involved with these organizations:

METRO TEEN AIDS
Metro TeenAIDS runs a diverse set of outreach, education, advocacy and community-level programs aimed at helping young people at risk of HIV infection and supporting those who are already affected by HIV/AIDS. (Chani is the youth ambassador for Metro Teen AIDS.)
http://www.MetroTeenAIDS.org

THE CENTERS FOR DISEASE CONTROL AND PREVENTION
(CDC), a part of the U.S. Department of Health and Human Services, is the primary Federal agency for conducting and supporting public health activities in the United States.
http:// www.cdc.gov

YMCA | The Nation's 2,686 YMCAs respond to critical social needs by drawing on our collective strength as of one of the largest not-for-profit community service organizations in the United States. Today's YMCAs serve thousands of U.S. communities, uniting 21 million children and adults of all ages, races, faiths, backgrounds, abilities and income levels. Our reach and impact can be seen in the millions of lives we touch every year.
http://www.ymca.net

THE BLACK AIDS INSTITUTE is the first Black HIV/AIDS policy center dedicated to reducing HIV/AIDS health disparities by mobilizing Black institutions and individuals in efforts to confront the epidemic in their communities. Our motto describes a commitment to self-preservation: "Our People, Our Problem, Our Solution." It is a non-profit, 501(c)(3) charitable organization based in Los Angeles, California.
http://www.BlackAIDS.org

Certificate of
Appreciation

This certificate is awarded to

Chantel Christie

in recognition of valuable contributions to
the community regarding HIV/AIDS Awareness

07-08 College of Arts and Sciences Student Council Executive President   Date

97-08 Mass College of Arts and Science   Date

11-17-07

Government of the District of Columbia

Certificate of Appreciation

IS HEREBY AWARDED TO

Chantel Christie

IN RECOGNITION OF YOUR OUTSTANDING COMMUNITY SUPPORT AND
DEDICATION RENDERED TO THE RESIDENTS OF THE DISTRICT OF COLUMBIA.
YOUR REPRESENTATION ON BEHALF OF OUR NATION'S CAPITAL AS A YOUTH
AMBASSADOR FOR HIV/AIDS AWARENESS HAS SET A STANDARD OF EXCELLENCE
FOR OTHERS TO EMULATE. YOU ARE AN INSPIRATION TO YOUNG WOMEN
NATIONWIDE AND YOUR EXCEPTIONAL SERVICE IS TO BE COMMENDED.

November 17, 2007

Mayor   Acting Secretary

Debut Album

http://www.chantelchristie.com

http://www.myspace.com/mychani

http://www.chantelchristie.com/fanclub.htm

Text "Chani" to 90101

Music Album | My Dream

1 Intro

2 Do You Dance

3 Crush

4 Who Is She

5 Young Love

6 Party

7 Chani's Story

8 Bowchicawowwow

9 Be That

10 I'm So Fly

11 New Boy

12 They Call Me Chani

13 Paparazzi

14 My Life

15 Enjoy the Ride

16 Girl Next Door

17 What's Going On

18 My Dream

19 Here We Are Again

MUSIC VIDEOS

Check out Chani's videos at:

www.ChantelChristie.com

1. *What's Going On?*
   (released in conjunction
   with this book)

2. *Chani's Story*

3. *Enjoy the Ride*

4. *Who is She?*

Chani childhood Photos

Six-years-old

Ten-years-old

Four-years-old

My Modeling ZED card

CHANTEL CHRISTIE

45.5" • Dress: 4/6 • Shoe: 12.5 • Hair: Black • Eyes: Brown

BRAND

My Modeling ZED card for my first agency

★ **Chantel Christie** ★

Hair: Brown **Eyes:** Brown
Date of Birth: 6-1-93

Photos By: The Studio/TB

United States Youth
Ambassador for HIV/AIDS

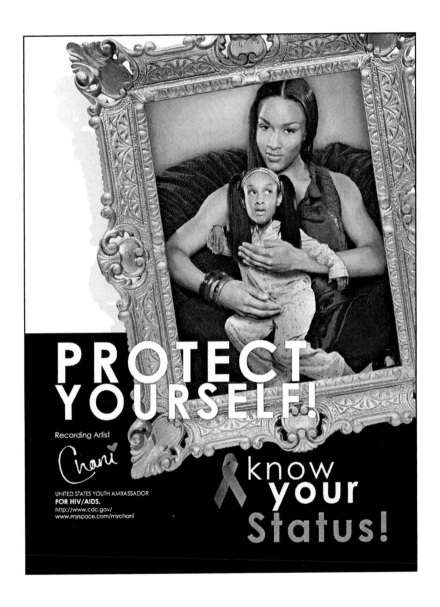

Chani ♥